LEARNING RESOURCES CENTER
UNIVERSITY OF WYOMING LIBRARIES
LARAMIE, WY 82071

Dorothy & Thomas Hoobler

YOUR RIGHT TO PRIVACY

Richard B. Morris, Consulting Editor

Franklin Watts   1986   A First Book
New York   London   Toronto   Sydney

Photographs courtesy of:
The Bettmann Archive: pp. 4, 9; AP/Wide World: 14, 56;
UPI/Bettmann Newsphotos: pp. 22, 47;
New York Public Library Picture Collection: p. 24;
Rolm Corporation: p. 33; U.S. Bureau of Census: p. 42.

Library of Congress Cataloging in Publication Data

Hoobler, Dorothy.
Your right to privacy.

(A First book)
Bibliography: p.
Includes index.
Summary: Surveys the concept of the right of privacy, its history, the laws protecting it, the effects of computers and other technological developments, and the conflict of the rights in such issues as national security and police investigations.
1. Privacy, Right of—United States—History—Juvenile literature. [1. Privacy, Right of]
I. Hoobler, Thomas. II. Morris, Richard Brandon, 1904–   . III. Title.
KF1262.Z9H66 1986   342.73′0858   85-31540
ISBN 0-531-10110-X   347.302858

Copyright © 1986 by Dorothy and Thomas Hoobler
All rights reserved
Printed in The United States of America
6 5 4 3 2 1

Contents

Chapter One
Do We Have a Right
to Privacy?
1

Chapter Two
The Technology of Spying:
From Telegraph to Satellites
12

Chapter Three
Who's Looking at You?
20

Chapter Four
Who's Got Your Name?
30

Chapter Five
Rights in Conflict
41

Chapter Six
Protecting Your Rights
51

Chapter Seven
The Future of Privacy
60

For Further Reading
63

Index
65

Your Right to Privacy

Chapter 1
Do We Have a Right to Privacy?

What is privacy? Most people think they know. When we go into a room and shut the door, that's a signal we want to be left alone. If you have a diary that you don't want others to look at, you might write PRIVATE on it. If you see that word on a door, you know it means "keep out." Most people feel that they have a right to privacy in their homes. When you close the door to your home, what goes on inside is your family's business. No one is supposed to look through your windows, put an eye to the keyhole, or break in.

But there are many other ways of violating your privacy. Modern technology has made it possible for someone to listen or look inside your home without ever coming near it. Today, people can tell about the private affairs of others by looking at records on paper or in computers. How far does the right to privacy extend? Does the right to privacy prevent the government from collecting information about you? Does a criminal planning a crime have a right to privacy? Does your employer have a right to know private things about you? Can your school look into your locker or pockets or purse? These are complicated questions. To answer them, we have to find out where the right to privacy came from.

The Origins of A Right to Privacy

In earlier days in England, the right to privacy was connected to the privacy of the home. In the British common law, the right to be secure in one's home was expressed thus: "The poorest man may in his cottage bid defiance to all the force of the Crown. It may be frail; its roof may shake; the wind may flow through it; the storms may enter, the rain may enter—but the King of England cannot enter; all his forces dare not cross the threshold of the ruined tenement!" The common law thus gave guarantees to protect against unreasonable government searches in homes.

The British common law was brought to the United States by the colonists and became the basis of much of the American legal system. The American colonists proudly asserted their rights as Englishpeople. In the troubled times before the American Revolution, the home country took actions that restricted these rights.

The English government took action to enforce harsh tax laws, prevent smuggling, and seize literature hostile to the crown. In order to do this, the English government gave officials unrestricted rights to conduct house-to-house searches. The colonists greatly resented these blanket search warrants, known as "writs of assistance." A Boston lawyer, James Otis, used his oratorical skill to protest the writs. Using the argument of common law, "A man's house is his castle," he lost his case in a court of law but won in the court of public opinion. Later, when the American Revolution created a new nation, the United States, people wanted a strong guarantee that their homes would be safe from such searches.

Although the Constitution does not mention the word *privacy*, it was thought that various parts of the Bill of Rights covered certain privacy rights. Most clearly, the Fourth Amendment guarantees "the right of the people to be secure in their persons, homes, papers and effects, against unreasonable searches and seizures." In the eighteenth century, when personal papers and effects were usually kept in the home or place of business, this seemed an adequate guarantee. In the two hundred years since the writing of the Bill of Rights, technology has made these guarantees less certain.

A Legal Definition of "Privacy"

"Privacy" as a legal term first arose in 1890, in an article in the *Harvard Law Review* by Samuel Warren and future Supreme Court Justice Louis Brandeis. The article arose from some incidents in Warren's personal life. He was a wealthy lawyer, with a luxurious home in the fashionable Back Bay section of Boston. His wife was a leading social figure and gave many parties. The sensational newspapers of the day liked to give their readers all the details of Mrs. Warren's parties, along with pictures of her guests. With the development of easy-to-carry cameras and telephoto lenses, reporters could snoop on the parties without actually trespassing on the Warrens' estate.

In their article, "The Right to Privacy," Warren and Brandeis defined "privacy" as the "general right of the individual to be left alone." They claimed that the rights to protection of property, life, and liberty should be broadened to "intangible" as well as

The Bill of Rights

ARTICLE I

Congress shall make no law respecting an establishment of religion, or prohibiting the free exercise thereof; or abridging the freedom of speech or of the press; or the right of the people peaceably to assemble and to petition the Government for a redress of grievances.

ARTICLE II

A well-regulated militia being necessary to the security of a free State, the right of the people to keep and bear arms shall not be infringed.

ARTICLE III

No soldier shall, in time of peace, be quartered in any house without the consent of the owner, nor in time of war but in a manner to be prescribed by law.

ARTICLE IV

The right of the people to be secure in their persons, houses, papers, and effects, against unreasonable searches and seizures, shall not be violated, and no warrants shall issue but upon probable cause, supported by oath or affirmation, and particularly describing the place to be searched, and the persons or things to be seized.

ARTICLE V

No person shall be held to answer for a capital or other infamous crime unless on presentment or indictment of a Grand Jury, except in cases arising in the land or naval forces, or in the militia, when in actual service, in time of war or public danger; nor shall any person be subject for the same offense to be twice put in jeopardy of life or limb; nor shall be compelled in any criminal case to be a witness against himself, nor be deprived of life, liberty, or property, without due process of law, nor shall private property be taken for public use without just compensation.

ARTICLE VI

In all criminal prosecutions, the accused shall enjoy the right to a speedy and public trial, by an impartial jury of the State and district wherein the crime shall have been committed, which districts shall have been previously ascertained by law, and to be informed of the nature and cause of the accusation; to be confronted with the witnesses against him; to have compulsory process for obtaining witnesses in his favor, and to have the assistance of counsel for his defense.

ARTICLE VII

In suits at common law, where the value in controversy shall exceed twenty dollars, the right of trial by jury shall be preserved, and no fact tried by a jury shall be otherwise re-examined in any court of the United States than according to the rules of the common law.

ARTICLE VIII

Excessive bail shall not be required, nor excessive fines imposed, nor cruel and unusual punishments inflicted.

ARTICLE IX

The enumeration in the Constitution of certain rights shall not be construed to deny or disparage others retained by the people.

ARTICLE X

The powers not delegated to the United States by the Constitution, nor prohibited by it to the States, are reserved to the States respectively, or to the people.

"tangible" possessions. The article argued, "The intensity and complexity of life . . . have rendered necessary some retreat from the world . . . so that solitude and privacy have become more essential to the individual." However, according to the authors, modern inventions "have, through invasions upon [people's] privacy, subjected [them] to mental pain and distress, far greater than could be inflicted by mere bodily injury."

Warren and Brandeis's article was the basis of the modern development of privacy law. In the years that followed, it was cited in many court cases dealing with privacy rights. Even Warren and Brandeis admitted that privacy was not totally guaranteed by the Constitution. They said that the right to privacy should receive added protection through passage of new laws. The years that followed did, indeed, see such new legislation.

The First Laws Protecting Privacy

Not everyone in the legal community agreed with Warren and Brandeis. In 1891, the Supreme Court of New York heard the first privacy case brought in that state. The issue was whether private citizens of a community had the right to erect a statue of a locally prominent woman. Her family was opposed, and they sued, claiming that the statue violated their right to privacy. The Court denied the family's claim.

However, the issue of privacy remained alive. In 1902, the case of *Roberson v. Rochester Folding Box Co.* came before the New York Court of Appeals. A flour company had used in its advertising the photograph of a young woman, Abigail Roberson, without her consent. Titled "Flour of the Family," the photograph was printed on the company's ads and put up in stores and other public places. In an age when nice young girls had their names in the newspaper only "at birth, at marriage, and at death," the advertisement made Ms. Roberson an object of jokes. She won a lawsuit against the flour company in a lower court, but the Court of Appeals reversed the verdict.

This outraged the public. It led to the first state law protecting privacy in New York in 1903. The law forbade anyone to make use of the name or picture of a person for "advertising purposes or purposes of trade" without written consent. Other states passed similar laws protecting individuals from commercial exploitation. In general, this principle still holds in today's law.

*The Supreme Court
Rules on Privacy*

Other state laws were passed protecting certain privacy rights, but the main issue raised by Warren and Brandeis remains controversial. Does the Constitution guarantee a general right to privacy? Since 1900, the Supreme Court of the United States has had numerous opportunities to rule on this question. Most of the cases have involved the tapping of telephone lines. Telephones were, of course, unknown at the time the Bill of Rights was written. This is a good example of the way courts try to apply traditional law to changing conditions of modern life.

The Fourth Amendment, with its guarantee of the right of people to be "secure" in their homes, has often been cited as a reason to make wiretapping illegal. Is it a violation of privacy to have your phone line tapped—by anyone? Or do the police, in order to prevent or solve a crime, have the right to listen in on private telephone lines?

For many years, the Supreme Court ruled that wiretapping was not a violation of the Fourth Amendment. In 1928 one important case that upheld this was *Olmstead v. United States.* Prohibition of alcoholic beverages was then the law of the land. Federal agents had tapped the office telephone of a suspected bootlegger to gather evidence against him. The majority of the Court, led by Chief Justice (and former President) William Howard Taft, said that the Fourth Amendment protected only against physical entry of the premises. Because the wiretap was made on a wire outside the defendant's office, it was not a violation of the Fourth Amendment.

Justice Brandeis Disagrees

Louis Brandeis was by this time an associate justice of the Court. He wrote a vigorous dissent in the *Olmstead* case. He pointed out that federal agents had violated a state law against wiretapping in gathering evidence against Olmstead. He said it was "immaterial" that the wiretap had not been physically conducted inside the defendant's office. Nor was it material that the defendant had in fact been guilty of bootlegging.

"Whenever a telephone line is tapped," Brandeis wrote, "the privacy of the persons at both ends of the line is invaded." At the time the Constitution was written, he wrote, force and violence were the only means of invading one's privacy. "Discovery and invention have made it possible for the government, by means far more effective than stretching upon the rack," to gain information about people. What was important was that the writers of the Constitution "sought to protect Americans in their beliefs, their thoughts, their emotions, and their sensations. They conferred . . . the right to be let alone—the most comprehensive of rights and the right most valued by civilized man."

Brandeis also condemned the federal agents' violation of a state law against wiretapping. He wrote, "Decency, security, and liberty alike demand that government officials shall be subjected to the same rules of conduct that are commands to the citizen. In a government of laws . . . [government] teaches the whole people by its example. Crime is contagious. If the government becomes a lawbreaker, it breeds contempt for law."

*Congress Forbids It,
But Wiretapping Goes On*

In 1934, a federal law was passed that said "no person . . . shall intercept any [electronic] communication." In 1937, the Supreme Court ruled that this included wiretapping. That would seem to have settled the issue, but the United States entered World War II in 1941. War is the greatest threat to any society, and it is the time when government is most tempted to violate its own laws on the grounds of national security. President Franklin Roosevelt urged Congress to repeal the ban on wiretapping. When Congress failed to act, he issued a secret order to the Justice Department allowing it to use wiretapping to detect enemy agents and spies.

Meanwhile, as Justice Brandeis had warned, new technology provided other ways to listen in on people's conversations. New kinds of privacy cases were brought to the Supreme Court. In 1942, it ruled that a listening device placed on the outer wall of a room by federal agents was legal. Once again, the reasoning was that

Louis Brandeis, Associate Justice of the Supreme Court, worried early on about technology's threat to privacy.

the device did not physically penetrate the room of the defendant. In a similar case, however, a "spike" microphone did penetrate a wall and touched the heating duct of a house. This, said the Court, was illegal.

The Court continued to argue over such fine distinctions. Dissenters on the Court argued that the issue was not the physical invasion of premises. It was, as Justice William Brennan said, the fact that "These devices . . . permit a degree of invasion of privacy that can only be described as frightening."

The Court Rules in Favor of Privacy

Finally, in 1967, the Supreme Court set aside the idea that only a physical entry was a violation of the Fourth Amendment. In the case of *Katz* v. *United States*, FBI agents had placed a listening device on the outer wall of a telephone booth. They recorded the conversations of a suspected gambler. Since the device was not inside the booth, the government's lawyers argued that it was not a violation of the Fourth Amendment.

A majority of the Court disagreed. Its decision stated that the "Fourth Amendment protects people, not places." The defendant, Katz, had entered the telephone booth in search of privacy. "One who occupies it, shuts the door behind him . . . is surely entitled to assume that the words will not be broadcast to the world," the Court's majority said.

However, the Court cautioned that it was not recognizing any "general constitutional 'right to privacy.' . . . A person's general right to privacy—his right to be let alone by other people—is . . . left largely to the law of the individual states." Nonetheless, the *Katz* decision was often cited in later cases as a precedent for the right to privacy.

The Issue of Privacy

Today, the issue is still muddled. Each of the fifty states has its own laws and regulations on privacy. As we will see, the Supreme Court has heard other cases about privacy issues. But is there a real right to privacy? That is still a hotly contested legal issue.

In 1974, Congress passed a Privacy Act. Section 2 of the act reads, "the Congress finds that . . . the right of privacy is a personal and fundamental right protected by the Constitution of the United States. . . ."

However, this right must be protected in specific laws. A broad declaration of the right of privacy can be interpreted in many ways by the courts. Only specific laws—local, state, and federal—can say what guarantees of privacy you have. The people, through their elected representatives, make the laws. If enough people feel strongly that a law ought to be passed, it usually is. This book will attempt to describe some of the issues of privacy that affect you today. Your decision on these matters will help make the laws of the future.

Chapter 2

The Technology of Spying: From Telegraph to Satellites

In their *Harvard Law Review* article, Warren and Brandeis spoke of recent inventions such as "instantaneous photographs" and "numerous mechanical devices" that made it necessary for the law to "recognize and protect the right to privacy." They could hardly have foreseen the twentieth century's technological discoveries—such as satellites, computers, and lasers—that threaten people's privacy today.

Early Uses of Technology

At the time the Constitution was written, people communicated through speech and written messages. The telegraph, the first form of long-distance electronic communication, was not developed until the 1830s. It wasn't long before someone discovered a way to "tap" into a telegraph line to intercept messages. The first government use of "wiretapping" was during the Civil War, to spy on messages of military importance.

The telegraph company, Western Union, was also the first private business to become involved in government's desire for information. After the disputed presidential election of 1876, there were many charges of vote fraud. A congressional committee was appointed to decide the winner of the election. It asked Western Union to give it copies of thirty thousand telegrams sent by important politicians during the election campaign. The president of Western Union refused. He was arrested and the telegrams were seized.

In 1876, Alexander Graham Bell invented the telephone. Almost immediately, devices were produced to allow others to listen in on conversations. During World War I, when the United States entered the war against Germany, American citizens of German descent were suspected of being spies. Local police departments began to tap the telephones of people with German names. An alarmed Congress passed a law banning wiretapping for the duration of the war. As we have seen, wiretapping by government agencies continued later.

These methods of investigating people's private lives were crude compared to those made possible by today's technology.

The Computer

The most powerful tool used by modern science is the computer. It was developed for military use during World War II. After the war, it became widely used by private businesses. As you will read in this book, your name is almost certainly kept on file in more than one computer already. A computer can be hooked up to other computers to compare and combine information about you.

Today, personal computers, sometimes costing less than $100, are available to anyone. A device called a modem can attach the

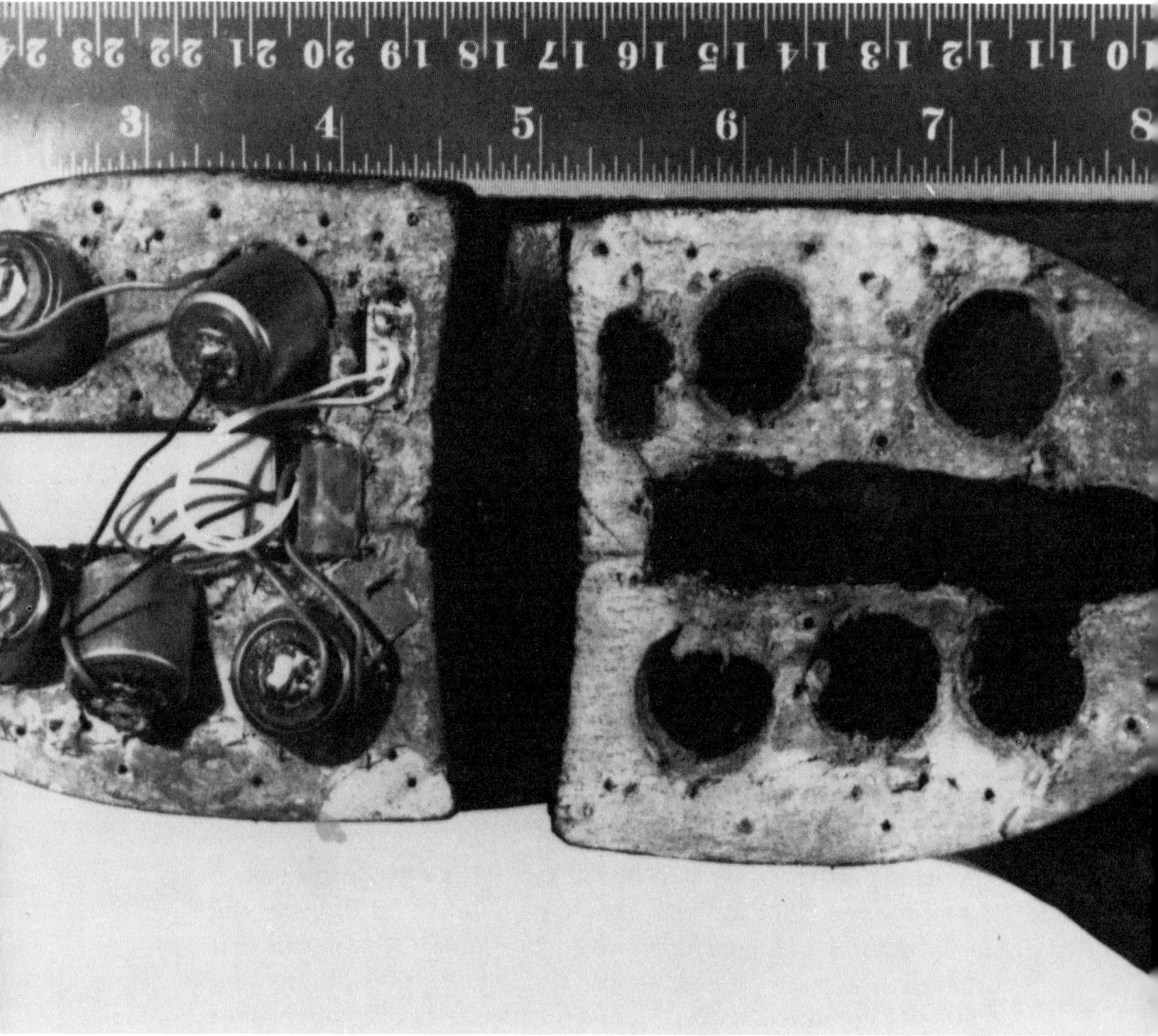

A radio transmitter can be placed even
in the heel of a man's shoe.

computer to a telephone. If a person knows the right number to call, the personal computer can then be linked up with other computers. Often, people link up a series of computers in this way to a "computer bulletin board." Messages can be left for other computer hobbyists.

But as we will see, some people have used their computer skills to look into the private affairs of others. Business and government computers can be used by anyone who knows the correct code or telephone number. A computer can be programmed to dial different numbers for hours until it finds the right one. In this way, computer "hackers" have found the secret access code numbers. They can then search computer records held by businesses or government agencies.

Listening Devices

It is no longer necessary to tap into a wire to listen in on a person's telephone calls. Many long-distance calls are carried by satellite. Electronic waves rise into space to an orbiting satellite, and are redirected to telephone company offices. With the right equipment, anyone can intercept these phone calls.

Furthermore, computers have been developed that can "listen" to thousands of telephone conversations at once. These computers can be programmed to recognize the "voiceprint" of a particular person. They can be instructed to respond to certain words, and pick out a conversation in which those words are used.

Conversations in a home or office are no longer secret. "Bugs," or hidden microphones, have become so tiny that they can be disguised as picture hooks. Laser beams aimed toward the window of a building can detect vibrations made by people speaking inside. The vibrations can be translated back into speech, for anyone to listen to or tape.

Tiny tape recorders can be carried by anyone wishing to record a conversation. Tapes are increasingly being used as evidence in criminal trials. They can also be placed secretly to overhear conversations.

Watching Devices

Satellites can also carry powerful telescopes to spy on areas of the earth. These can be useful to governments wishing to collect information on other countries. From thousands of miles out in space, these satellites can "see" and photograph objects as small as a golf ball. However, a government can also use satellite telescopes to spy on its own people.

Darkness is no protection against the spying eyes. Infrared film can "see" anything in a darkened room. The heat given off by human bodies can be sensed by special TV cameras. These have been set up at the borders of the United States to detect people trying to enter the country illegally. Many worry that they can also be used to track people going about their everyday lives.

Lie Detectors

Both businesses and police have often made use of the polygraph, or lie detector. Supposedly, the machine can tell when a person is giving a false answer to questions. In reality, the machine only records changes in a person's pulse, blood pressure, breathing, perspiration, and skin temperature. The operator of the machine must then interpret these changes to tell if a person is lying.

New types of lie detectors measure "voice stress," using slight changes in a person's tone of voice to tell if he or she is telling the truth. Voice stress tests have the added advantage that the subject is not aware of the test. Yet another machine measures the size of the pupil of a person's eye as he or she is asked a question. This machine tells a person's reaction to a question, even if he or she refuses to answer.

There is much disagreement as to how accurate these "lie detector" methods are. The Congressional Subcommittee on Information and Individual Rights said that "there is no 'lie detector,' neither machine nor human. People have been deceived by a myth that a metal box in the hands of an investigator can detect truth or falsehood." Some experts claim that a particularly nervous person will show up as "lying," even when telling the truth. Some say that carefully trained people can fool lie detectors by remaining calm, even when they are lying.

Other experts insist that these machines can indeed tell when a person is not telling the truth. All agree that the accuracy of the machine depends on the skill of the person operating it.

Tom Hemmert worked for a grocery store in Lima, Ohio. A shortage of $1,000 was found in the store, and all employees were asked to take lie detector tests. Hemmert willingly agreed. One of the questions he was asked was, "Do you know who took the money?" Hemmert had suspicions about the thief, but had no real proof. He hesitated when answering the question. Because of this, the store fired him. His labor union took up the case, and he was eventually given his job back.

Psychological Testing

The lie detector is one way technology has provided of looking inside your head, the ultimate violation of privacy. Some kinds of tests, called psychological tests, also give others ways to tell what you *might* do.

Businesses, government, and schools all use psychological tests. Businesses use them to tell if a person is likely to be a good employee, or if a person can handle a more responsible job. The tests are usually written, although they can be given in the form of spoken questions. The answers people give to the questions are supposed to indicate what kind of employees they would be.

Most people for example, would answer no if they were directly asked, "Would you steal if given the chance?" but psychological tests often describe a situation and then ask the tested people to tell their reactions: "Was this person treated fairly?" "Was this an honest thing to do?" "Which person did you think was right?" The answers a person gives may tell if he or she is likely to steal.

Psychological tests often ask very personal questions about religion, politics, home life, and other details of the person's life. Many people have complained that the employer has no right to know these things. Schools give psychological tests too, and similar objections have been raised to their use.

Another kind of test is a graphoanalysis test. This takes a sample of a person's handwriting. An expert known as a graphologist analyzes the handwriting and gives a report on the person's character traits from it. This kind of test is widely used in some European countries, and is becoming more popular in the United States. Since no personal questions are asked, it is thought to be less of an invasion of privacy than the psychological tests. But its reliability has been questioned.

As of now, there are few laws telling businesses what kinds of tests they can perform on their employees. If a job applicant "fails" a test, he or she has no way of appealing the result. Usually, the company just denies them a job without saying why. Those who refuse to take such tests will, of course, be denied employment.

Drug Testing

Drug abuse has become a serious problem in recent years. Businesses want to know if their employees are taking drugs that could hurt their job performance. They often demand that employees take chemical tests that detect the presence of drugs in urine. It has been said that about 25 percent of the five hundred largest companies in the U.S. require such tests.

In 1985, the commissioner of major league baseball, Peter Ueberroth, proposed that all baseball employees take such tests, except for the players. The players' agreement with the club owners forbids such testing, but Ueberroth hoped that players would voluntarily take the tests.

Experts disagree as to how accurate drug tests are. Dr. David Greenblatt, of the Tufts New England Medical Center, said of the most commonly used drug test, "False positives can range up to 25 percent or higher. The test is essentially worthless."

Others point out that the test may show if a person has taken drugs anytime in the past several days. This would cover time when the person was not actually on the job. Some people have questioned whether companies should have the right to determine the conduct of their employees while off the job, so long as they can carry out their duties normally.

Chapter 3

Who's Looking at You?

A lot of people want to learn about you. With the methods described in the previous chapter, they can find out a lot. Who uses these methods? For what kinds of information do they look?

Police Investigations

First of all, the police often look into the affairs of citizens to solve or prevent crimes. Since most people don't consider themselves criminals (and you probably don't!), they tend to look on police investigation as a reasonable invasion of privacy. Honest citizens don't think the police would investigate them.

However, the police often consider it their right to investigate just about anyone. And for one reason or another, you might be on their list. As we've seen, during World War I, police in some places began to investigate anyone with German names. That was why Congress passed a law preventing wiretapping during the war. With the war's end, police wiretapping resumed, except in a few states that passed laws against it.

Later, after World War II, suspicion fell on Americans who were suspected of communist activity. Police once more began to investigate large groups of people. A congressional committee found that the New York police department had tapped the phone lines of more than a hundred thousand homes and offices. In Philadelphia, the phones of union leaders and liberal lawyers were tapped. In California, the movie industry came under suspicion. Local police listened in on the telephones of Hollywood stars and producers. Even elected officials were subject to police wiretaps if they had liberal or leftist views.

The 1960s were a time of social ferment. Blacks began to organize to demand equal rights with whites. Later in the decade, protests against the United States' involvement in the Vietnam War were widespread. Demonstrators for these and other causes marched in the streets or gathered together to show their views. Peaceable public demonstrations are a legal way of expressing one's views. Yet police departments photographed demonstrators and drew up lists of people who took part in public protests.

Police departments also use TV cameras in public places to prevent crime. The Capitol building in Washington has more than a hundred cameras to watch suspected terrorists. Some police departments have set up cameras on city streets in high-crime areas. These are controlled by an operator in police headquarters who can "follow" a suspicious person or zoom in to get a closeup look.

Police also use computers to exchange lists of suspicious people with other police departments. Sometimes people have gotten on these lists just because they belong to organizations that have unpopular political views.

Many states have passed laws against police surveillance techniques such as wiretapping. In general, these laws require a court order by a judge to permit the police to place a wiretap or other

Remote control TV cameras
"watch" a busy street.

spying device. The police have to show cause, or good reason, why a person should be placed under surveillance. If the police obtain evidence through surveillance without a court order, it can be thrown out in a trial. This frequently happens, indicating that police still use illegal means of investigating the affairs of citizens.

The Federal Government Watches Its People

The federal government itself has often cited national emergencies as a reason to investigate citizens' lives. During World War I, the Justice Department continued to use wiretaps to investigate citizens suspected of being enemy agents, even though Congress passed a law against it.

After World War I, the country saw a "Red Scare." The Communist Revolution in Russia caused a fear of socialists in the United States. These included many labor organizers. Attorney General A. Mitchell Palmer sent agents to raid homes and union halls in many cities. About four thousand men and women were arrested and held without charge and without access to lawyers. In one city, anyone who wanted to visit a prisoner was arrested as well. Palmer claimed that he was trying to ward off a communist revolution, but only three revolvers were found in the raids.

J. Edgar Hoover was one of Palmer's assistants at the time of the Red Scare. Hoover later headed the Federal Bureau of Investigation from 1924 to 1972. He became the nation's most famous law enforcement officer. The FBI's skill at apprehending bank robbers, kidnappers, and other criminals was widely publicized. Hoover was also a zealous anticommunist. He used the Bureau to investigate anyone suspected of having communist leanings. (It should be remembered that it is not illegal to be a communist.)

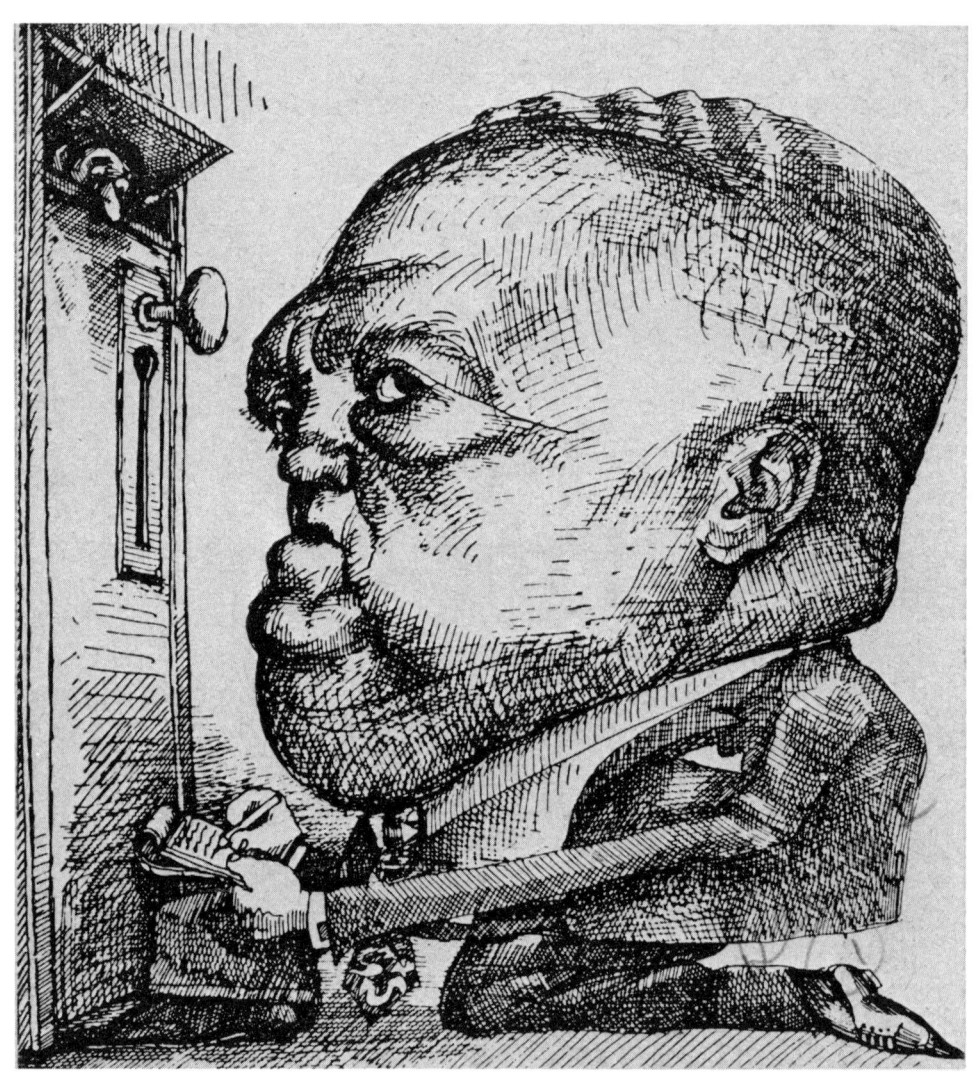

For a half century, J. Edgar Hoover, as head of the Federal Bureau of Investigation, was one of the most powerful men in the United States.

The FBI under Hoover kept watch on such groups as the National Association for the Advancement of Colored People (NAACP), the American Civil Liberties Union, the women's liberation movement, and even religious organizations. None of these groups had any connection with communism. Hoover had them investigated merely because he did not like their views.

Congressional hearings in the 1970s showed that the FBI illegally opened mail, wiretapped telephone conversations, and even conducted burglaries to gather information. Sometimes the FBI sent letters to the employers of suspected people, resulting in their being fired from their jobs. The legal rights of thousands of innocent citizens were violated by the FBI during this period.

Hoover also investigated people whose social ideas he thought dangerous. Among these was Dr. Martin Luther King, Jr. During King's leadership of the black civil rights movement, the FBI often tapped his phones and bugged his home and hotel rooms.

Over the years, the FBI has kept files on millions of American citizens. A file might be opened because of a newspaper article about a person, or a complaint by a coworker or neighbor.

Hoover extended his investigations to government officials, including presidents. He kept numerous files on political leaders, with details of their private lives that were often embarrassing. Hoover used this information to increase his own power and that of the FBI.

After Hoover's death in 1972, the FBI's illegal activities were curtailed. Lately, there have been signs that it has begun again. The Reagan administration has been concerned about the threat of the leftist government in Nicaragua. FBI officials have contacted Americans returning from Nicaragua and confiscated some of their papers. Americans who opposed the U.S. government's policy toward Nicaragua have claimed that their mail has been opened.

There are other government agencies whose chief job is spying. The best known of these is the Central Intelligence Agency (CIA). Its main job was intended to be gathering information about foreign countries. The charter of the CIA forbids it to spy on American citizens. However, congressional hearings in the mid-1970s revealed that the CIA had been opening the mail of U.S. citizens for at least ten years. Furthermore, the CIA had kept illegal files on thousands of American citizens.

The Nixon Administration

During the administration of Richard Nixon, government spying reached its height. Nixon's close aides drew up an "enemies list" that included the names of people who simply opposed Nixon's policies. Newspaper columnists, politicians, sports stars, and entertainers were on the list. Nixon sought to use the FBI and other government agencies to harass these people. He ordered the Internal Revenue Service, the tax-collecting agency, to conduct audits of some of their tax returns.

Some of Nixon's orders alarmed even Hoover. The FBI director refused to cooperate with Nixon's plans, and the White House formed its own unit of investigators, called "the Plumbers." A former government official "leaked" to the press copies of the Pentagon Papers, a government study of the Vietnam War. Nixon's Plumbers broke into the office of the man's psychiatrist to find out information about him.

Later, Nixon's reelection committee was found to have placed illegal wiretaps in Democratic Party headquarters in the Watergate apartment complex. When Nixon's role in covering up the Watergate affair became known, he was forced to resign.

The federal government legally collects a great deal of information about its citizens. Every citizen must fill out a tax return. Nearly everyone must have a Social Security card to get a job. The government takes a Census every ten years and asks numerous questions about the lives of its people. There are good reasons for the collection of this information. But as the examples of Hoover and the Nixon administration show, there is always the possibility that this information will be used to control political activity.

Business and Schools Are Watching You

Private businesses also use surveillance techniques. If you walk into a bank, you can often see a TV camera's eye pointing at you, recording your face on videotape. In some supermarkets and department stores, TV cameras and two-way mirrors allow security people to watch you shop—or shoplift.

Shoplifting by employees is a serious problem for some businesses. They have been known to set up TV cameras to spy on employees in stock rooms or rest rooms.

Schools, as you know, also keep watch on their students. Sometimes they set rules of dress and conduct for students. Some people claim that these rules have sometimes violated students' rights to privacy. In the late 1960s, an Iowa school suspended three of its students for wearing black armbands to protest the Vietnam War. The case went to court, and it eventually was heard before the Supreme Court. In 1969, the Court ruled in favor of the student. It said that students did not "shed their constitutional rights of freedom of speech . . . at the schoolhouse gates."

In this case, the decision was based on the students' First

Amendment right of free speech. That is a different right from privacy. The court did not rule as to whether schools have a right to violate students' privacy by setting standards of dress and behavior. Since the 1969 case, lower courts have ruled that if a student's conduct or dress is disruptive to classroom work, then the school does have the right to discipline the student.

Schools have also claimed the right to look into students' lockers and desks, or even search them physically. These searches are usually made to find stolen property, weapons, or drugs. In March 1980, a junior high school student in New Jersey was accused of smoking in the school bathroom. School officials searched her purse, found marijuana in it and called in the police.

In the court cases that followed, the girl was identified as "T.L.O." to protect her identity. T.L.O.'s lawyer claimed that the school had no reason to search her without "probable cause" that she had committed a crime. This case too went to the Supreme Court, which in 1985 ruled in favor of the school. In its ruling in the case of *New Jersey* v. *T.L.O.*, the Court agreed that the Fourth Amendment requires probable cause in police searches. But the Court ruled that teachers and school officials need only "reasonable grounds" to search a student. The Court said that reasonable grounds were present in this case, but did not give guidelines as to what reasonable grounds for other searches might be.

Anybody Can Look

You read in Chapter 2 of many kinds of devices that can be used to invade people's privacy. Most of these are easily obtained by ordinary people. Some of them are advertised in magazines. There is no way to know how many people are spying on others using these devices. Their use is difficult to detect.

A Nassau County, New York, businessman was sentenced to jail for a year for secretly recording the telephone conversations of a female employee and her boyfriend. He was doing this for amusement, replaying the tapes for his friends.

Even more powerful than bugging devices is the computer. In the movie *War Games*, a young computer whiz (called a "hacker") used his home computer to change his grades on the school computer. Then he nearly started a war when he electronically broke into a government computer. This was only a story, but computer crime is a very real problem.

There have been many reports of young computer hackers actually breaking into government or business computers. In 1985, seven young people were arrested for using their home computers to exchange stolen credit card numbers. Using these numbers, they ordered merchandise that was sent to a post office box. Someone else—the owner of the credit card—was billed for the merchandise. These same young people were also reported to have obtained secret telephone numbers to break into computers in the Defense Department. Perhaps *War Games* might come true.

As you will learn in Chapter 4, your name is already on file in a number of computers. Computers today are the giant filing cabinets of business and government. Imagine what a hacker could learn about people by breaking into the computers that hold their records. On a giant scale, this is like someone being able to look through your most private papers—without your ever knowing about it. The computer may be the most widespread and powerful way for people to "look at" you, and find out what you're doing.

Many of the reports of computer snooping have involved young people. However, there is no reason to think that adults or private groups are not using computers in the same way to investigate people's lives.

Chapter 4
Who's Got Your Name?

When John Hancock stepped forward to sign the Declaration of Independence in 1776, he signed it in unusually large and elaborate fashion. He said he wanted King George III of England to "be able to read it without his glasses." The founders of our country were breaking the laws of England, and they boldly put their names to the document that established "a new nation, conceived in liberty." None of them could have dreamed of the countless ways that people's names could be collected for all sorts of reasons at the present time.

Your Name Is Already in the Files

No matter how young you are, the government and many businesses already have collected your name. When you were born, the name your parents gave you was registered with your city or state. Your birth certificate is proof that you are a United States citizen. You'll need it if you ever apply for a passport to travel to a foreign country. It's proof that you are a native-born American should you ever decide to run for president.

If you were baptized in a church, there is a record of that on file. It can substitute for a birth certificate in some cases.

Many local newspapers print a list of local births, and if you look through the back files, you can probably find your name. Some businesses collect these lists and then try to sell parents products meant for babies and children.

Your parent or guardian probably fills out an income tax form every year. The federal income tax forms asks them to list the names of their children and other dependents. So does the Census held every tenth year. Your name is already on file with the federal government.

Your school also keeps records on all its students. It has your grades, and in many cases includes the results of IQ tests, psychological tests, and comments made by teachers about you. Laws give you the right to obtain these records, when you are an adult. However, if you apply for a job someday, your employer can also ask for these records.

You may not have held a job yet. But when you do, your employer will ask for your Social Security number. Most businesses have to withhold part of your pay for taxes and Social Security payments. If you don't have a Social Security card, you'll have to apply to the government for one. You'll also use your Social Security number when you fill out your own income tax form. Your first income tax return will open a file in your name in the Internal Revenue Service.

If you're a male, the federal government currently requires

you to register your name when you turn eighteen. If there is a need for men to be drafted into the Army, Congress may authorize a draft. Your name will then go on the list of those eligible.

Who Else Will Get Your Name in Your Life?

These are only the things you have to do. Sometime in your life, you may wish to have a credit card or borrow money from a bank to buy a car or house. Banks and stores require applicants for loans or credit cards to fill out a form. This usually asks a series of questions about the applicant's job, income, and home. Then, your name will go into a computer that will check it against many other lists. Banks, businesses, and even private individuals such as landlords and doctors make their computer records available to other groups.

Today, computers make it possible for a worker at a desk to type in your name and find out all sorts of information about you. This information will follow you throughout your life. If you don't pay a bill, it goes on the computer. If you get a parking ticket or are arrested for speeding, the computer will remember.

There are today large credit bureaus that collect information about people. When you apply for a credit card or loan, the bank checks with the credit bureau. The credit bureau sends the bank all the information it has about you. This may include private information other than financial records. Just one of these companies, Credit Bureau Inc., has more than a hundred million names on file.

Credit bureaus are not the only agencies that keep files on people. The Medical Information Bureau has files on over ten million Americans. This information is made available to over

Computers are everywhere, aiding, protecting, and monitoring people's activities.

seven hundred insurance companies that want to know if people are good insurance risks.

This is legal, and serves a purpose. People who have borrowed money and not repaid it can't get another loan. People who don't pay their bills are marked as bad credit risks. The trouble is, sometimes there is false information about you on the computer.

The Computer Doesn't Lie— or Does It?

Computer experts like to say that computers don't make mistakes. This is usually true, because the computer is just a machine with a big memory. But people put information into computers, and people do make mistakes.

The editor of *Changing Times* magazine found that a credit bureau listed his occupation as "changing tires." A bank officer began to receive notices that he was behind on his credit card payments. He found out that his file had gotten mixed up with the file of a house painter with the same name.

Many people have had the experience of receiving a bill for something they didn't buy. The person operating the computer typed in the wrong name or number. In this situation, people often have trouble correcting the mistake. If they refuse to pay the bill and send a letter explaining why, it may be ignored. A second bill arrives, and then a third, and then a threatening letter (also sent by a computer). While you're trying to straighten out the problem, a credit bureau may receive the report that you haven't paid your bill on time. Eventually, you may convince the store that you didn't buy what you were billed for. But the credit bureau still has the bad report on you. It will send it to the next place you apply to for a credit card or loan. It is often hard to track down and correct the mistake.

False information about you may deliberately be placed on your credit report. In June 1982, the Federal Trade Commission brought charges against Equifax, a major credit bureau. The FTC showed that Equifax encouraged employees to turn up unfavorable information about people they were checking. One employee admitted that he had made up unfavorable information about people to make it seem he had been doing a good job of investigating. A court declared that Equifax had not violated any law.

The Electronic Future

More and more, banks are turning to "electronic banking" as a way of doing business. Customers are given special cards with a magnetic strip on the back. This can be placed in a banking machine at any hour to deposit or withdraw money, or move money from one account to another. In many banks, customers can "hook up" to the bank's computer with a computer at home. Customers can check on their account, or move money from one account to another. In most cases, the customer has a secret code or password that lets the bank's computer know the right person is using the card or account. But if another person learns your secret code number or word, they can easily fool the computer.

Another innovation brought about by computers is "electronic mail." Instead of writing a letter and sending it through the post office, businesses and individuals can use a computer to send a message to another computer.

Both electronic banking records and electronic mail messages are kept in the computer's memory. There, they can be called up and read by employees who know the code—or even by computer experts from outside. In 1983, some teenagers in Milwaukee broke into the Telenet electronic mail system. They freely read the messages that were stored there. Computer crime is so new that police could find no law that made this illegal.

Cable television is becoming more popular. People can get better TV reception on cable. They can also watch programs that are not available on commercial TV. Some new cable TV systems even let the viewer "talk back." They have conducted polls on how viewers like a certain program. The viewer presses a button on the cable box at home to answer. Cable TV companies can learn other things about viewers' likes and dislikes. The threat to privacy is that there is no law against their selling this information to other companies, who may want to sell products.

What Does Your School Say about You to Others?

Schools, as you know, keep records on their students. They include not only grades, but also comments made by teachers. A school counselor may give you a psychological test. The results of these go on the school records. Sometimes schools give intelligence tests that are supposed to measure how smart you are. Many people question the use of these tests. They say a psychological test can be affected by how you felt that day. Intelligence tests may not give a real estimate of your abilities. They may tell more about the kind of home you grew up in. Many people who scored low on these tests have gone on to become outstanding successes.

All your records are kept by the school for many years. In the past, neither students nor their parents were allowed to see these records. Congress changed that in the Family Educational Rights and Privacy Act of 1974. (See Chapter 6.)

However, many people feel that schools are allowed to send their records to too many people. Many employers routinely ask for school files on people who apply for a job. The federal government can look at your school file. Is it important for them to know what your fifth-grade teacher might have thought about you? Should they be allowed to judge you on the basis of an intelligence test you took while you had a bad cold or headache? Should the opinion of one school counselor be allowed to follow you throughout your lifetime?

Fifteen Files on You— and Everyone Else

The biggest collector of information is the federal government. All federal agencies combined have over three and a half *billion* files on the citizens of the United States. This is an average of fifteen files for each living person in the U.S. Even the most powerful computers are unable to easily handle all this information.

In addition, no one knows if much of this information is true or false. Government investigators often ask friends, neighbors, and coworkers about people. A person who dislikes you may give false information. But the information goes into your government file anyway. Honest mistakes also can go uncorrected.

In 1985, a Michigan man, Terry Dean Rogan, sued the city of Los Angeles. He claimed that he had been arrested five times in fourteen months because the Los Angeles police department had put his name on the FBI computer file of wanted criminals. But Mr. Rogan had never committed a crime. He had lost his wallet in 1981. It contained his driver's license and other ID cards. A man with Mr. Rogan's IDs was later suspected of committing several crimes in Los Angeles. That was when a warrant for his arrest was first sent out.

The FBI's computer file can be a great help in catching criminals. Police departments all over the country can check it to see if a suspected person is wanted anywhere else. Many police cars are now equipped with a hookup to this computer. When police in Michigan did a routine traffic check, they stopped Mr. Rogan's car. They saw his name on the FBI computer and arrested him. Even though he could easily prove his innocence, Mr. Rogan was arrested five times in similar ways. FBI officials said there are problems removing flawed records from the system.

Is this an isolated case? Perhaps not. A study by Congress's Office of Technology Assessment found that about one out of five of the warrant records in the FBI file was false.

Anybody Can Start
a File on you

Just as any private person can use technology to spy on you, private groups can, and do, also collect files on people. Most of these groups back a particular political viewpoint, and collect information on citizens that they think are suspicious or disloyal. This is a particularly dangerous form of information collecting, because there is no legal check on how these files can be used or who they can be shown to.

During the 1950s, many people in the United States became concerned about the threat of communists to the security of the country. Senator Joseph McCarthy used his power to accuse many people of being communists, or communist "sympathizers." The mere accusation was often enough for a person to lose his or her job.

At that time, private groups compiled lists of people that they claimed were "subversives." The most important of these was the American Business Consultants (ABC). ABC published a manual called *Red Channels: Report of Communist Influence in Radio and Television*. If a person's name was listed in this book, it became impossible for him or her to get a job in the broadcasting field.

After Senator McCarthy was censured by the Senate, the anticommunist hysteria died down. But there are still many private groups that compile lists of people they believe are dangerous or subversive. The Church League of America says it has a counter-subversive file of seven million index cards that is "the most reliable, comprehensive, and complete, second only to those of the FBI."

The American Security Council (ASC) has a file with more than six million entries. A critic of the ASC says it keeps the file up to date through informer reports, government documents, and newspaper and magazine clippings. It makes its files available to businesses which want to know if employees belong to "questionable" organizations or have worked for certain kinds of political causes. Yet there is no way of checking how reliable these files are.

Other private information-collecting organizations exist. Some have been accused of gathering information through illegal means, including wiretapping, burglary, and infiltration of political groups.

*Do You Want a Name—
or a Number?*

Recently, there has been a proposal to use the Social Security number to keep track of everyone from birth to death. At birth, a child would be given a number, and that number would be placed on all his or her records in school, business, and government.

This card would have many uses. It would help solve the problem of illegal immigrants. A person could not walk out on unpaid bills by moving to another part of the country. A person with a secret bank account or other secret assets could not collect government assistance. Wanted criminals could be easily identified and captured if they had to give their ID number to rent a room or buy anything that couldn't be paid for in cash.

Many countries already have a national ID card of this kind. Some people say this is one reason why crime rates in other countries are generally lower than in the U.S.

But Americans have always resisted this kind of government control of their affairs. Would you like to give your ID number to take a plane ride, buy a car or house, go to a doctor, or enter a new school? Would you like all the records about you, from birth to death, put in one huge file in a government agency? Is there a danger that computer hackers could gain access to the file? Is there a danger that some future government would try to restrict the rights of its people by using such files? As with most questions about privacy, people must balance the advantages of information-gathering against the dangers of it. You will read about this conflict of rights in the next chapter.

Chapter 5
Rights in Conflict

Few people would claim that the right to privacy is absolute. The police must look into private homes to investigate crimes. If a government is to collect taxes, it must know something about its citizens' financial affairs. Businesses need to know something about the people they hire. Banks and other financial institutions must ask questions about the finances of people who borrow money. Schools must maintain order if they are to do a good job of teaching students.

Today, people expect government to help them in many ways. The federal government builds interstate highways, passes pollution control laws, operates the Social Security system, and gives aid to states and cities. To carry out these and many other tasks, it has to collect information on how its citizens live. The Census, taken every ten years, is one legal way of collecting this information. Every citizen is required to answer the questions the Census takers ask. On a random basis, some citizens answer a great many questions about themselves, their families, and the way they live. The

*Every ten years, when the population is counted,
the government collects more and more information.*

government must have answers to these questions to determine what kinds of government action are needed.

National Security

To many, the greatest need of society is its security. People today are troubled by crime, by the threat of foreign enemies, and by internal dissension. Some would argue that any violation of privacy is allowable if it helps promote security.

President Nixon defended many of his actions on the grounds of national security. However, when people found that he had tried to cover up the link between his reelection committee and the burglary of Democratic Party headquarters, Nixon had to resign. The Democratic Party is a mainstream political group, one of the two major political parties. People felt that spying on it was going too far.

But there are other groups whose political views are less popular. The antiwar demonstrations during the Vietnam War frightened many people. Some individuals and groups resorted to violent actions. In response, the FBI, the CIA, and even the U.S. Army carried out illegal break-ins and surveillance against protesters. Many people would have argued that these activities were necessary. But they were still kept secret because they were illegal.

The Constitution gives rights to all citizens, not just those whose views are popular. If government is allowed to illegally spy on even one person, it opens the way to spying on everyone. Justice Brandeis, in the *Olmstead* case, put it this way: "Experience should teach us to be most on our guard to protect liberty when the government's purposes are beneficent. Men born to freedom are naturally alert to . . . invasion to their liberty by evil-minded rulers. The greatest dangers to liberty lurk in insidious encroachment by men of zeal, well-meaning, but without understanding."

Yet there are real threats to national security. Some recent cases of spying were uncovered through use of the kinds of surveillance you have read about. In July 1985, John A. Walker, Jr., a former U.S. Navy man, was accused with members of his family of providing secret information to the USSR. Prosecutors in the case revealed that wiretaps and other electronic surveillance helped federal agents crack the spy ring. However, it appears that the wiretaps were approved by a judge, as the law demands.

A Defense Department report released in 1985 said that polygraph, or "lie detector," tests had recently caused nine people holding sensitive government jobs to admit that they had agreed to spy for foreign countries. In the same year, a polygraph test discovered that a CIA employee in the U.S. embassy in Ghana was giving away secret information. Combined with the Walker case, this disclosure caused members of Congress to propose a law requiring polygraph testing of everyone cleared to receive "top secret" information.

In fact, the CIA and National Security Agency already have the power to require employees to take polygraph tests. Private defense contractors, whose employees also have access to secret information, also began giving polygraph tests in 1985. Yet government officials say that so much secret information passes through the hands of so many people that it is impossible to test them all.

Leaks

The federal government has often shown the desire to use surveillance techniques to solve lesser problems. In nearly every presidential administration of the last twenty years, the problem of "leaks" has been raised. A leak occurs when a government employee or official gives supposedly secret information to a journalist. The purpose of the "leaker" is not to betray the country, but to expose what he or she believes to be a serious problem that people need to know about. The leak is often embarrassing to the government, and both Republican and Democratic administrations have sought to stop them.

The Reagan administration has required that any government employee submit to a lie detector test. In one case in 1982, a writer for the Washington *Post* revealed information from a Defense Department meeting. The information was that President Reagan's defense budgets might cost $750 billion more over five years than the administration claimed. This was information that taxpayers needed to know. Nonetheless, the Defense Department gave a polygraph test to everyone who had been at the meeting. One person "flunked" the test, and was fired. The employee fought the decision and managed to keep his job. Later, the Washington *Post* reporter who wrote the original story revealed that the man who failed the polygraph test was not the person who gave him the secret information.

There are many questions about government actions against spies and subversives. How far can government investigation go before it violates the rights of innocent people? Does government sometimes use national security as an excuse to keep the people from knowing things that they should know about their government? Are too many documents marked "secret" just because a government doesn't want its own citizens to know about them?

The Problem of Terrorism

Terrorism has recently become a serious problem in the world. Everyone has read about the airplane hijackings carried out by terrorists to force their demands on governments. To counter the problem, airlines require passengers to pass through metal detectors and send their luggage through X-ray machines at airports. Virtually everyone agrees that such measures, though violations of privacy, are necessary for the safety of all.

The threat of terrorism can cause government to take other measures that infringe on people's rights. In 1983, FBI agents put video transmitters into the houses of suspected members of the Puerto Rican terrorist group FALN. They observed people making time bombs and learned that the bombs were to be used to blow up military bases. However, a District Court judge threw out the videotape evidence. He said that, "no one, not even in the name of ferreting out crime, has the right to invade the privacy of a home" without proper legal authority. In 1985, however, a higher court ruled that the video surveillance was proper and legal. This case illustrates the confusion that new kinds of technology have brought to the field of privacy law. The case has now been appealed to the Supreme Court.

Police Surveillance

Police departments have the job of catching criminals. Most police officials would like to use any means available to them to do this job. Many citizens would agree. Again, however, the conflict of rights arises when the police violate the rights of many people to find those few who may break the law. Was it necessary for the New York Police Department to tap the phones of a hundred thousand people to discover a very few lawbreakers? Is it necessary for the police to set up video cameras to watch all citizens going about their business? Citizens must make up their own minds because in our country the citizens control what the police can do.

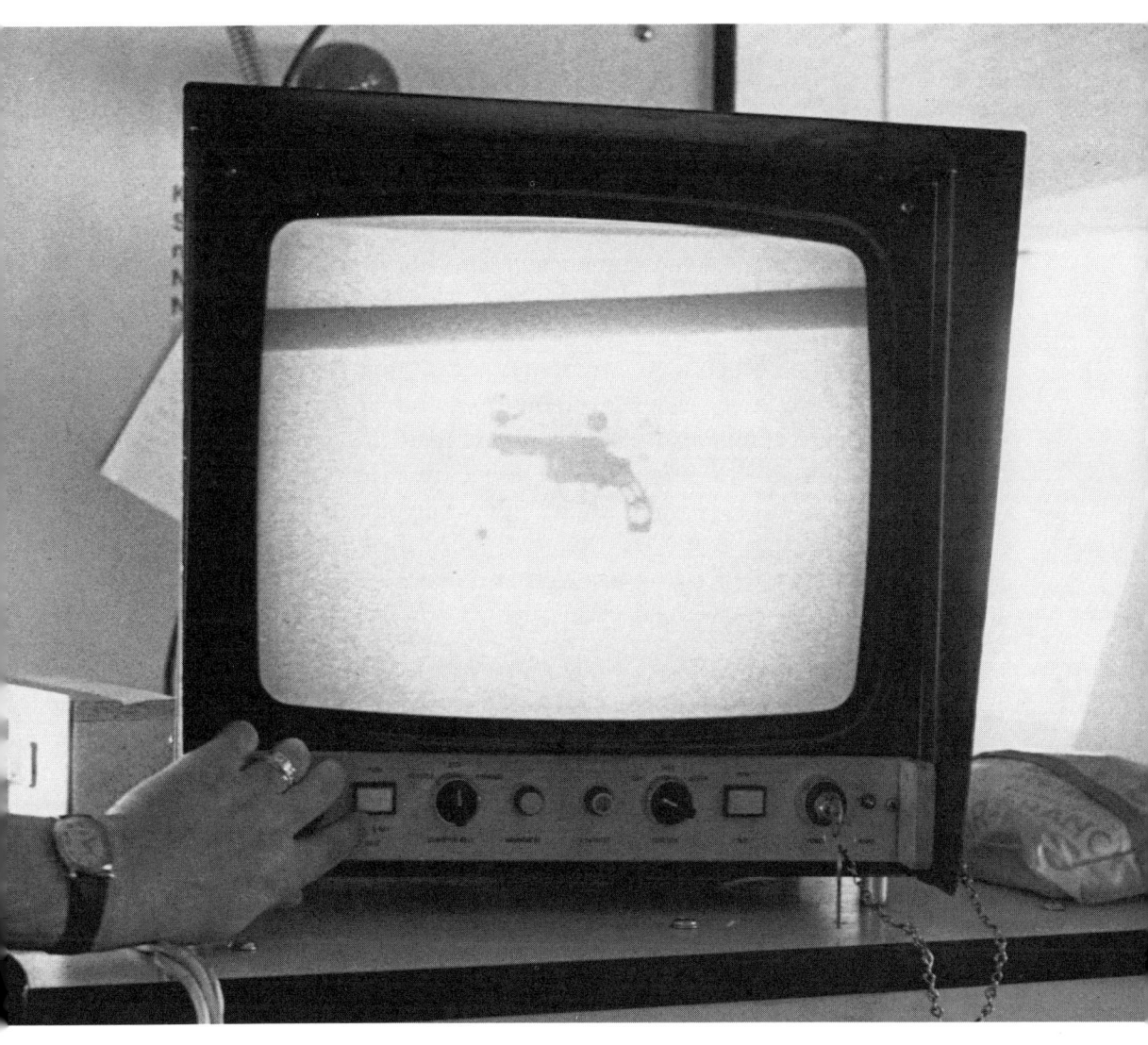

At Athens International Airport, police test
a metal detector unit.

The writer George Orwell wrote a famous novel called *1984*. He described a society in which the leader, "Big Brother," has agents spying on everyone. The society is an orderly one. There is no crime, not even "thought-crime," because even thoughts can be detected.

The year 1984 has come and gone. Big Brother is not here, but he exists in countries like the Soviet Union, where people are sent to insane asylums because they oppose the policies of the government. When a government has the right to enter people's homes at any time, or spy on them in any way it thinks necessary, crime is less common. But freedoms are reduced too. Somewhere, there is a line between legitimate police investigation of criminals and Big Brother. No one knows just where that line is. That is why the courts have ruled that the police must respect constitutional rights when trying to catch criminals.

Who Should Have the Right to Investigate You?

Violations of privacy by businesses, banks, schools, and private groups present another conflict of rights. The federal government, as you will see in the next chapter, has passed some laws to help people correct mistakes about them in credit reports and school records. Yet most businesses, schools, and private groups can violate people's privacy without breaking any law.

There are good reasons for this. Businesses must have the right to set standards for the people they hire. Schools must maintain order to do a good job of teaching all students. Banks cannot give credit to people who are not likely to pay their bills.

Yet banks and businesses, as we have seen, have increased their power to look into people's lives. In our society, most people work for a company or business. Do they have to give up their rights to privacy when they take a job? Do students give up their rights when they go to school? These are hard questions to answer.

Most people would think that a business does not have the right to ask any question it wants about a person's private life. Yet some businesses regularly ask whether a person has ever seen a psychiatrist, taken drugs, or been arrested. In many cases, it is not necessary to know these things to tell if a person would make a good employee. It would be difficult to write a law that described exactly what questions a business could ask, and which kinds it could not.

Stores also have the right to protect themselves against shoplifting. It is difficult to say how far they can go before they violate the rights of their customers. In 1985, a pregnant woman was shopping in a sporting goods store in a shopping mall in Virginia. After she left the store, security guards in the mall stopped her. They took her back to the store, where she was accused of shoplifting. The guards were convinced that she was hiding a basketball under her blouse. They threatened to have her arrested. In front of several male guards and store employees, she was forced to remove her sweater and lift her blouse to show that she was really pregnant. She sued the store.

This may be an unusual case, but it is a fact that most large stores routinely use hidden TV cameras and two-way mirrors to watch their customers. To many people, this seems too much like the world of Orwell's *1984*. Yet the stores argue that they must do these things to prevent shoplifting. Does a person lose the right to privacy when entering a store? There is no simple answer.

Passing laws against the kinds of information a private group can ask for presents many problems. In April 1985, Paul Trout, a fifteen-year-old Boy Scout in West Virginia, applied for the rank of Life Scout. He had been a Scout since the age of eight and had completed the requirements in the Scout handbook. But the local Scout Council asked him about his religious beliefs and his ideas about Creation. He answered that he respected the rights of others to believe in God as a "Supreme Being," but did not hold such a belief himself.

The Scout Council refused to give him the rank of Life Scout. The national Boy Scout office defended this action. It said that one of the requirements of being a Boy Scout was "belief in a Supreme Being." The boy was expelled from his local Scout troop.

After an analysis of the matter, the national executive board of the Boy Scouts voted to delete from the organization's literature the definition of God as a "Supreme Being." The Scout oath, with its mention of God, stands, but each youngster individually remains free to decide what that means. On October 10, after affirming that he could subscribe to the Boy Scout oath and law, Paul Trout received his Life Scout promotion.

Trout said he had not planned to sue the Boy Scouts. It is difficult to say what a court would have ruled on the matter. You be the judge. Did the Boy Scouts have the right to ask such a question? Did they have the right to demand certain religious beliefs for membership in a nonreligious organization? Were the boy's rights to privacy being violated? Different answers to any of these questions might be defended.

The right to privacy often comes into conflict with other rights and needs of society. Modern life is far more complicated and dangerous than the writers of the Constitution could have foreseen. Warren and Brandeis proposed a "right to privacy" in response to the changed conditions of their day. Citizens today must again look at their society and decide how valuable privacy is to them.

Chapter 6

Protecting Your Rights

To protect your own right to privacy, you must be informed about your legal rights. In some cases, laws do protect your rights. In other cases, no laws protect certain kinds of invasions of privacy.

The Freedom of Information and Privacy Acts

Most laws protecting privacy have been passed to protect citizens against government investigation. As early as the 1960s, there was public concern over the vast number of files that the federal government collected on the people of the U.S. In 1966, Congress passed the Freedom of Information Act. Basically, this gave citizens the right to ask a federal agency for any files it had about them. The law had many loopholes, and in 1974 a new law, the Privacy Act, was passed. It set a limit on the time a federal agency had to respond to a request for files. It required that all information in a person's files had to be "timely" and "accurate." However, government agencies were allowed to withhold certain kinds of information they had in a person's file.

Many people used the Freedom of Information Act to uncover false reports about them, some many years old, in government files. Penn Kimball, a professor at the Columbia School of Journalism, was one who asked for his files. He found out that over many years' time, the FBI and other agencies had collected unfavorable comments about him. Most of these said that he was "far to the Left" or even procommunist. Kimball had been an Eagle Scout, Rhodes scholar, and respected journalist. He had worked as an aide to some prominent politicians. None of the accusations against him included any proof. Yet Kimball was surprised to learn that the Kennedy administration had considered appointing him to a job but decided not to on the basis of this secret file. At no time had Kimball been given any chance to respond to the file's unfavorable comments; in fact, he had never even known of its existence.

Kimball had the time and money to pursue the search for his file. It took him six years to obtain it. However, most people are not able to obtain their government files, despite the Freedom of Information Act. Some government agencies dragged their feet in enforcing the law. Some people received copies of reports with important information blacked out. Often, this concerned the source of the information in the government files. (By refusing to reveal the names of informants, the government is protecting their privacy.)

A citizen has a right to go to court to force disclosure of files, but this can be time-consuming, expensive, and discouraging. Also, government agencies have the right to charge for the time it takes to find a person's file, and to make duplicate copies of it. This cost is usually not high, but it can be.

At the time the Freedom of Information Act was passed, some people feared that its regulations would hamper legitimate government efforts to protect national security. There has been no case in which disclosure of files has been shown to harm national security.

The Fair Credit Reporting Act

Alarmed by the dangers involved in computerized private credit checks, Congress passed the Fair Credit Reporting Act of 1970. It said that most information that was more than seven years old had to be deleted from credit bureau files. It also said that a business ordering a credit check on someone must inform the person in writing within three days. The person being investigated has the right to request and receive additional information about the check. If the person is denied credit, insurance, or employment as a result of the check, he or she has the right to find out the reasons why. The law also gives a person the right to point out false information in the report, and the right to ask for a new investigation. Finally, any person who is still dissatisfied with the new report may attach to the report a statement explaining his or her side of the dispute.

The Family Educational Rights and Privacy Act

To protect school records, Congress also passed in 1974 the Family Educational Rights and Privacy Act. This gave students over eighteen years old the right to see their records, if their school received federal funds. The parents of a student under eighteen could ask for school records. The law said that if there was false information in the records, a student could ask for a hearing to present his or her case. If the school authorities denied the need for a change, then the student could attach a statement to the record. School officials were also required to keep a log of the outside requests made for a student's records. There had to be a good reason for sending records to outside parties.

Here again, there were loopholes in the laws. A school guidance counselor was allowed to ask students to sign a statement that they will never ask to see letters of recommendation written by teachers about them. Some people argued that records were still allowed to be sent to too many other agencies. These agencies, such as testing and research bureaus, might then disclose the records to other people without restraint. There may be information about you on many computers, without your knowledge.

Federal Laws Regulating Banking

In 1970, Congress passed the Bank Secrecy Act. This increased the availability of people's banking records, a significant invasion of privacy. The Act required banks to keep complete records of all transactions. Among other things, banks were required to microfilm the front and back of every check written by their customers. These records were to be kept for five years. Government agencies were given access to these records. The purpose was to allow the government to discover people who were cheating on their taxes, or writing checks for other illegal purposes.

Over time, Congress changed its mind about bank secrecy. Republicans and Democrats alike thought that opening a person's financial records in this way was a violation of privacy. In 1978, Congress passed a new law, the Right of Financial Privacy Act. This required government agencies to inform people before investigating their bank accounts. But critics say that the 1978 act did not go far enough. Banks still keep all financial transactions on record. Whenever information like this exists, it is possible for people to use it for illegal means or to persecute people who have unpopular ideas.

The Privacy Protection Study Commission

President Jimmy Carter appointed a Privacy Protection Study Commission in 1977. This committee issued a report that warned against the widespread collection of information in and out of government. It said that the laws did not give a citizen "the tools he needs to protect his legitimate interest in the records organizations keep about him."

The Privacy Commission recommended that new laws be passed. One would prevent an employer from using polygraphs or other equipment to test an employee. Another recommendation was that people should have a right to see and copy all information gathered about them by credit bureaus. New limits were recommended on the use of information gathered by federal agencies.

However, Congress did not carry out the recommendations of the Privacy Commission. No new federal laws protecting the individual right to privacy have been passed since 1978. However, there have been some new privacy laws passed by the states.

Your Employer and Your Privacy

Few laws exist to protect an employee against invasions of privacy by his or her employer. As you have read, there are many ways for employers to look into the lives of their workers. There are no

federal laws against this type of privacy invasion. Some states have passed laws limiting what employers can do. But the situation is bleak for employees who want to protect their privacy.

The American Civil Liberties Union is an organization that works to protect people's rights. It has published a book, *The Rights of Employees*. These are some of the questions discussed:

1. Must I take a "lie detector" test, if asked, to get or keep a job?
2. Can I be required to take a psychological or personality test to get a job?
3. Can my employer use electronic surveillance?
4. Can my employer search me or my personal effects?
5. Can I be required to submit to fingerprinting, tests, etc.?
6. Can an employer do a credit check on me?
7. Can an employer inquire about my personal life?
8. Can an employer require me to meet certain dress and grooming standards?

The answer to all these questions is yes or "generally, yes." A number of states and the District of Columbia prohibit an employer from requiring you to take a "lie detector" test. Some states prohibit the asking of certain kinds of questions on the test.

However, you cannot see your personal file in most states. Your employer can disclose information about you to other people, including those outside the company.

A polygraph instrument tests the truthfulness of answers given by employees or potential employees.

School Searches

As you have read, the Supreme Court ruled in 1985 that schools need only "reasonable grounds" to search students. After the ruling, an incident in Elyria, Ohio, showed how some schools may make use of this ruling.

At Westwood Junior High School in Elyria, a girl reported that her watch and ring were missing. She thought she had left them in the girls' locker room. The girls' gym teacher searched the lockers of the twenty other girls in the class. When nothing was found, a male assistant principal told the girls that they had to be searched.

The girls were all seventh-graders. The assistant principal told them that if they didn't let female school employees search them, he would call the sheriff. The sheriff would then search them. The girls allowed themselves to be searched.

They were ordered to strip to their underwear in front of the female gym teacher, a secretary, and a guidance counselor. When nothing was found in their clothing, the women looked inside their bras. The watch and ring were never found.

The girls who were searched were deeply upset. Some of their parents decided to sue the school and some of its employees. Two local newspapers wrote editorials condemning the search. One editorial said, "If Elyria's teachers are led to believe . . . that they have the community's blessings to continue such Gestapo tactics at their own will and whim, there is something dangerously flawed in the community's attitudes toward personal liberty and privacy." But the superintendent of schools defended the search, citing the authority given by the Supreme Court in *New Jersey* v. *T.L.O.*

In this particular case, the threat to call the sheriff was probably an empty one. A police officer would probably not have the power to search a group of people under such circumstances. Some parents in Elyria suggested that their children had the right to call their parents in the case of such a search. But it is hard for schoolchildren to insist on their rights in such a situation.

The girls' lawsuit has not yet been settled. It too may eventually go to the Supreme Court. But again, you can be the judge. School officials said that the search was necessary because one of the girls was likely to have the watch and ring. Others argue that theft is not an excuse to violate the privacy of twenty schoolchildren in such a manner. Who was right?

Chapter 7

The Future of Privacy

As you read in Chapter 1, it was invasions of privacy by newspaper reporters that caused Warren and Brandeis to write their article on privacy in 1890. Today, investigations by press, radio, and television still violate people's rights.

The Constitution guarantees freedom of the press. In general, today's media, including radio and TV, exercise this right freely. But people are often offended by the sight of TV reporters sticking a microphone into the face of a person who has just suffered a terrible tragedy and asking, "How do you feel?" This seems like the ultimate violation of privacy, yet such scenes are broadcast almost daily.

The interesting thing is, however, that most people answer the question. Have you ever seen a person respond to a TV reporter: "That's none of your business!" (Of course, that may be because people who give such a response aren't put on the air.)

People seem very willing to have their privacy violated, especially if it brings them a few moments of fame. In the 1970s, a

California family allowed cameras to follow them around for weeks in the making of a TV documentary. In the course of the TV series, the most personal things about the family were shown. The husband and wife actually decided to get a divorce, while cameras and microphones recorded their conversation.

We have become used to the idea that television news can bring us almost instantly pictures of terrible events in the lives of people. When millions view the most intimate moments of people's lives on television, the idea spreads that privacy isn't such an important matter. It seems to become a public right to know about others. Such scenes may blunt people's sensitivity to their own privacy.

How do Americans actually feel about privacy? In February 1984, the Gallup poll showed that 47 percent of Americans "believe they now have little or no privacy because our government can learn anything it wants about them. An additional 19 percent say it is very likely we may lose the right to privacy."

In a Harris poll of December 1983, 84 percent of those polled said they thought it would be fairly easy for someone to compile a master file about their lives.

In fact, there are probably greater safeguards of privacy rights in the United States than in any other country. But history shows that rights can be eroded if people are not willing to fight for them. One of the frightening things about the society of Orwell's *1984* was that most people felt it was useless to resist government control of their lives. If most people feel the right to privacy cannot be maintained in the face of giant computers and modern technology, then privacy may well be a doomed right.

As we have seen, many of the laws passed by Congress to protect privacy came at a time when people were very concerned about protecting this right. In times when people are less wary, rights can be endangered. Also, as we have seen, threats to the nation can cause government leaders to set aside their respect for privacy. Terrorism, spies, and crime are threats that people worry about today. These can easily be used by government leaders as an excuse for violating the privacy of all. And people may well agree that privacy must be a secondary right. Except in revolutions, rights do not disappear overnight. As Justice Brandeis said, people "born to freedom" are more on guard against invasions of their liberty by "evil-minded rulers." The greater threat to privacy comes from "men of zeal, well-meaning, but without understanding."

A full understanding of the reasons for or against privacy cannot be given by this one small book. Safeguarding rights depends on people who seek to inform themselves on the issues. People must be willing to fight for, and demand rights that they think are needed. The future of the right to privacy depends on how important it seems to citizens. The future of privacy depends on you.

For Further Reading

Bamford, James. *The Puzzle Palace*. New York: Penguin Books, 1983.

Breckenridge, Adam Carlyle. *The Right to Privacy*. Lincoln, Nebraska: University of Nebraska Press, 1970.

Donner, Frank J. *The Age of Surveillance*. New York: Vintage Books, 1981.

Dorsen, Norman, ed. *Our Endangered Rights*. New York: Pantheon Books, 1984.

Goode, Stephen. *The Right to Privacy*. New York: Franklin Watts, 1983.

Hayden, Trudy, and Novik, Jack. *Your Rights to Privacy*. New York: Avon Books, 1980. Tells how to take action against inaccurate credit ratings, correct your medical and school records, and apply for your government files under the Freedom of Information and Privacy acts.

Marwick, Christine M. *Your Right to Government Information.* New York: Bantam Books, 1985. Gives up-to-date information on how to use the Freedom of Information and Privacy acts to protect your rights.

Outten, Wayne N., and Kinigstein, Noah A. *The Rights of Employees.* New York: Bantam Books, 1984. A full description of the current legal rights of nongovernment employees.

Rowan, Ford, *Technospies.* New York: Putnam's, 1978. A detailed look at the uses of computers and other kinds of technology to invade people's privacy.

Severn, Bill. *The Right to Privacy.* New York: Ives Washburn, 1973.

Smith, Robert Ellis. *Workrights.* New York: E.P. Dutton, 1983.

Westin, Alan F., and Salisbury, Stephan, eds. *Individual Rights in the Corporation.* New York: Pantheon Books, 1980.

Index

Advertising, 6
Airplane hijackings, 45–46
American Business Consultants, 39
American Civil Liberties Union, 25, 57
American Security Council, 39

Bank Secrecy Act of 1970, 54
Banks, 35, 41, 48, 54
Baptismal certificates, 31
Baseball, 19
Bell, Alexander Graham, 13
Bill of Rights, 3
    First Amendment, 27–28
    Fourth Amendment, 3, 6–7, 10
Birth certificates, 31
Boy Scouts of America, 50
Brandeis, Louis, 3–6, 7, 8, 12, 43, 50, 60, 62
Brennan, William, 10
Bugs. *See* Microphones

Carter, Jimmy, President, 55
Census, 27, 31, 41
Central Intelligence Agency (CIA), 26, 43, 44
Church League of America, 39
Civil rights movement, 21
Civil War, 12
Communists, 21, 23–25, 38

Computers, 1, 12, 13, 21, 34–38, 61
    hackers, 15, 29, 40
    modem, 13–15
Congressional Subcommittee on Information and Individual Rights, 17
Constitution, 3, 5, 6, 7, 43, 50, 60
Credit bureaus, 32, 34, 35, 48, 53, 55, 57
Credit cards, 29, 32
Criminals, 1, 25, 39, 40, 62
    computer hackers, 15, 29, 35–36, 40

Drug testing, 19

Employers, 1–2, 15, 16, 18, 19, 27, 31, 53, 55–57

Fair Credit Reporting Act of 1970, 53
FALN (terrorist group), 46
Family Educational Rights and Privacy Act of 1974, 53–54
Federal Bureau of Investigation (FBI), 10, 23–26, 37–38, 39, 43, 46
Federal government, 1, 11, 18, 23–27, 30–32, 37–39, 41, 44–45, 48, 61, 62
Federal Trade Commission, 35
Fingerprinting, 57
Freedom of Information Act of 1966, 51–53

Graphoanalysis tests, 18
Greenblatt, David, 19

Hoover, J. Edgar, 23–27

Immigration, 16, 40
Infrared film, 16
Insurance companies, 34, 53
Internal Revenue Service, 26, 31

Katz v. *United States*, 10–11

Lasers, 12, 15
Lie detectors. *See* Polygraphs.

McCarthy, Joseph, 38–39
Mail, 25, 26, 35–36
Medical Information Bureau, 32–34
Metal detectors, 46
Microphones, 10, 15
Military draft, 32

National Association for the Advancement of Colored People (NAACP), 25
National Security Agency, 44
New Jersey v. *T.L.O.*, 28, 58
Nicaragua, 25
Nixon, Richard, President, 26, 27, 43

Olmstead v. *United States*, 7, 43–44
Orwell, George. (*1984*). 48, 49, 61
Otis, James, 2

Palmer, A. Mitchell, 23
Passports, 31
Pentagon Papers, 26
Police, 6, 16, 20–23, 28, 38, 41, 46–48
Polygraphs, 16–17, 44, 45, 55, 57
Privacy Act of 1974, 11, 51–52
Privacy Protection Study Commission, 1977, 55
Psychological testing, 17–18, 31, 36, 57

Reagan, Ronald, President, 25, 45
Red Channels: Report of Communist Influence in Radio and Television, 39
Right of Financial Privacy Act, 1978, 54–55

Rights of Employees, The, 57
"Right to Privacy, The" 3–6, 12
Roberson v. *Rochester Folding Box Co.*, 5–6
Roosevelt, Franklin, President, 8

Satellites, 12, 15, 16
Schools, 1, 18, 27–28, 31, 36–37, 40, 41, 48, 54, 58–59
Search warrants, 2, 23, 28
Security,
 home, 2, 6, 10, 23, 41, 57, 61
 national, 8, 23–27, 29, 43–45
Shoplifting, 27, 49
Social Security number, 27, 31, 39–40, 41
Soviet Union, 44, 48
Spies, 13, 23, 25–26, 62
State legislation, 5, 7, 10, 20, 21–22, 57

Taft, William Howard, President, 7
Tape recorders, 16
Telegraph, 12
Telephones, 6, 13, 15, 25, 29
Telescopes, 16
Television, 16, 21, 27, 36, 46, 49, 60, 61
Terrorists, 21, 45–46, 62

Ueberroth, Peter, 19
U.S. Supreme Court, 6–7, 8, 10, 11, 27, 28, 58–59

Vietnam War, 21, 26, 27
Voice stress tests, 16
Voiceprints, 15

Walker, John A., 44
War Games (movie), 29
Warren, Samuel, 3–6, 12, 50, 60
Watergate affair, 26, 43
Western Union, 13
Wiretapping, 6–7, 8, 12, 13, 20, 21, 25, 26, 39, 44
Women's liberation movement, 25
World War I, 13, 20, 23
World War II, 8, 13, 21
Writs of assistance, 2

X-ray machines, 46